FROM SEA to SHINING SEA

PUERTO RICO

MICHAEL BURGAN

Consultants

MELISSA N. MATUSEVICH, PH.D.

Curriculum and Instruction Specialist
Blacksburg, Virginia

RAMÓN BOSQUE-PÉREZ

Center for Puerto Rican Studies
Hunter College
New York, New York

CHILDREN'S PRESS®

A DIVISION OF SCHOLASTIC INC.

New York • Toronto • London • Auckland • Sydney • Mexico City
New Delhi • Hong Kong • Danbury, Connecticut

Puerto Rico is an island in the Caribbean Sea.

The photograph on the front cover shows La Fortaleza and El Morro lighthouse in Old San Juan.

Project Editor: Meredith DeSousa
Art Director: Marie O'Neill
Photo Researcher: Marybeth Kavanagh
Design: Robin West, Ox and Company, Inc.
Page 6 map and recipe art: Susan Hunt Yule
All other maps: XNR Productions, Inc.

Library of Congress Cataloging-in-Publication Data
Burgan, Michael.
Puerto Rico / by Michael Burgan.
        p. cm. — (From sea to shining sea)
    Includes bibliographical references and index.
        Contents: Introducing Borikben — The land of Puerto Rico — Puerto Rico
through history — Governing Puerto Rico — The people and places of Puerto Rico —
Puerto Rico almanac — Timeline — Gallery of famous Puerto Ricans.
        ISBN 0-516-22398-4
        1. Puerto Rico—Juvenile literature. [1. Puerto Rico.] I. Title. II. Series.
F1958.3.B873 2003
972.95—dc21

                                2003008478

TABLE of CONTENTS

CHAPTER ONE

INTRODUCING BORIKÉN

A rainbow appears over Sun Bay beach on Vieques, an island of Puerto Rico.

An island sits in the Caribbean Sea, far off the coast of the United States. The weather there is usually sunny and warm. Along the island's shores are beautiful beaches, where tourists come to relax. Inland, the island has mountains and a rain forest. Rare birds and other creatures make their homes among the thick vines and trees.

Bienvenidos (welcome) to Puerto Rico! Puerto Rico has been part of the United States since 1898. If it were a state, Puerto Rico would be the third smallest, larger than only Rhode Island and Delaware. However, Puerto Rico is not a state; it is called a commonwealth. Some states are also called commonwealths, but Puerto Rico has a special relationship with the United States.

In some ways, Puerto Rico acts as an independent nation. It has its own constitution, as the United States does. This document spells out Puerto Rico's basic laws. The United States government, however, has some control over how Puerto Rico is ruled. The United States also defends Puerto Rico in case of war and handles its relations with foreign countries.

Before 1898, Puerto Rico was ruled by Spain for almost four hundred years. The Spanish influence is still strong in Puerto Rico. Today, Spanish and English are both official languages. In fact, the island's name is Spanish for "rich port." When the Spanish first arrived near what is now San Juan, they realized the area had a fine harbor where ships could easily dock.

The Spanish also brought African slaves to Puerto Rico. The Spanish sometimes had children with the slaves and with the island's native people, the Taíno. The Taíno called their homeland *Borikén,* meaning "land of the brave lord." Other Europeans also settled on Puerto Rico. The cultures of all these people blended to form a distinct, new culture.

What comes to mind when you think of Puerto Rico?

* Sandy beaches along warm, blue waters
* El Yunque, a tropical rain forest filled with fascinating wildlife
* Sugarcane, coffee, mangoes, pineapples, and other warm-weather crops
* Fast-paced salsa music, filled with drums and horns
* The cobblestone streets and mighty fortresses of Old San Juan
* Colorful street festivals with dancing and lots of food

Today, Puerto Ricans are proud of the culture created by the mixture of people who settled on their island. Although they are United States citizens, they are proud to call themselves Puerto Ricans.

San Juan

Bayamón • • Carolina

Ponce

ZOOLÓGICO

©SHY03

CHAPTER TWO

THE LAND OF PUERTO RICO

Puerto Rico is part of a group of four islands called the Greater Antilles. These islands form part of a larger island group called the West Indies. These islands circle the Caribbean Sea. To the north and east is the Atlantic Ocean. The Caribbean Sea separates North and South America, east of Mexico.

Puerto Rico is about 1,000 miles (1,609 kilometers) southeast of Florida. The island's closest neighbors to the west are the Dominican Republic and Haiti, which share the island of Hispaniola. To the east, the nearest islands are the U.S. and British Virgin Islands. Puerto Rico and the other Greater Antilles were created more than 130 million years ago by erupting volcanoes. Hot, liquid rock called lava poured out of the volcanoes and cooled to form the islands.

Today, Puerto Rico sits near one of the world's deepest ocean trenches. Trenches are V-shaped holes in the ocean floor. The Puerto Rico Trench plunges down more than 28,000 feet (8,540 meters).

Unusual limestone formations lie along the coast at Point Tuna.

Although rugged Mona Island has no permanent human inhabitants, many rare animal species live there, including endangered sea turtles and giant iguanas.

FIND OUT MORE

Trenches are formed when huge areas of rock in the earth, called plates, crash together. What is the world's deepest trench, and where is it located?

Shaped somewhat like a rectangle, the main island of Puerto Rico is about three times as long as it is wide. The territory of Puerto Rico also includes several smaller islands. The most important are Vieques and Culebra, on the east coast, and Mona on the west coast. In total, Puerto Rico covers 3,515 square miles (9,104 square kilometers).

Much of Puerto Rico is covered with hills and mountains. The mixture of high and low spots help define the island's land regions. Puerto Rico has two major regions—the coastal lowlands and the mountains. A smaller area with a unique land feature is sometimes called the Karst region.

COASTAL LOWLANDS

The coasts of Puerto Rico are mostly flat and are called lowlands, because they are close to the level of the sea. Most Puerto Ricans live in the northern coastal lowlands. This region is also the site of most major industry on the island.

The southern coastal lowlands are much drier than the northern coast. Mountains in the center of the island prevent much rain from reaching this region. Some dry areas, dotted with cactus, almost look like a desert, but they still receive some rain. Sugarcane is grown in parts of the south that receive the most rain. The much smaller eastern and western coastal lowlands also have farming. All the coastal lowlands have beaches, though most tourists visit the northern and southern coasts.

The coastal lowlands extend 2 to 8 miles (3 to 19 km) inland from the coast.

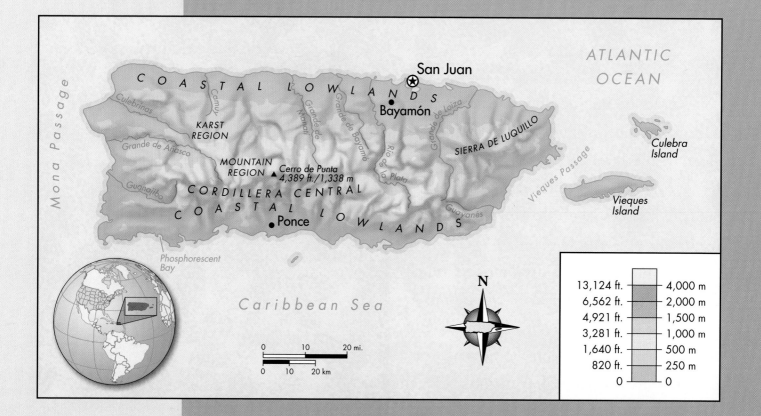

ATLANTIC
OCEAN

Mona Passage

C O A S T A L   L O W L A N D S

San Juan

Bayamón

Culebrinas

Camuy

Grande de Manati

Grande de

Grande de Bayamó

Grande de Loiza

KARST
REGION

Grande de Añasco

MOUNTAIN
REGION ▲ Cerro de Punta
4,389 ft./1,338 m

Río de la Plata

SIERRA DE LUQUILLO

Guanajibo

C O R D I L L E R A   C E N T R A L

C O A S T A L   L O W L A N D S

Ponce

Guayanés

Vieques Passage

Culebra
Island

Vieques
Island

Phosphorescent
Bay

Caribbean Sea

N

0   10   20 mi.

0   10   20 km

13,124 ft. — 4,000 m
6,562 ft. — 2,000 m
4,921 ft. — 1,500 m
3,281 ft. — 1,000 m
1,640 ft. — 500 m
820 ft. — 250 m
0 — 0

THE MOUNTAINS

Moving away from the coast toward the island's center, the land becomes hilly. This region, sometimes called the foothills, is also used for farming. Fruits and vegetables grow in this region.

Farther inland, Puerto Rico has two major mountain ranges. The largest is the Cordillera Central. It stretches for about 60 miles (97 km) across the southern part of the middle of the island. Puerto Rico's highest peak, Cerro de Punta, is located there. The mountain reaches 4,389 feet (1,338 m).

The second important range, the Sierra de Luquillo, is in the island's northeast corner. In these mountains is the Caribbean National Forest. It is also called El Yunque, the name of a mountain in the forest. El Yunque is a tropical rain forest. This kind of forest receives more than 100 inches (254 centimeters) of rain each year and features trees with high, thick leaves. Tropical means it is located in the tropics, a warm region that circles the middle of Earth. El Yunque is the only tropical rain forest under the control of the United States Park Service. As a national forest, El Yunque is protected, and certain activities, such as

The Caribbean National Forest grows on El Yunque Peak, part of the Luquillo Mountains in Puerto Rico.

The name of the tree frog—coquí (pronounced *koh-KEE*)—imitates the sound they make.

riding motorcycles or fishing, are not allowed. The forest has more than 240 types of trees and more than 60 kinds of birds. Visitors to the rain forest can hear the familiar cry of the coquí. This tree frog is found only in Puerto Rico.

KARST REGION

In Puerto Rico, the Karst region is in the northwest part of the island, near the town of Arecibo. Karst refers to a special land feature. Karst appears when limestone, a kind of rock, is worn away by rain. In some places, the worn rock creates large holes in the ground. Small hills are left around these "sinkholes," with caves and tunnels underneath them. The Karst region looks like few other places

Smoothly rounded hills and sinkholes characterize the Karst region.

on Earth, and many people find it beautiful. To make sure this land never changes, the Puerto Rican government has set aside several forests in the region. As in El Yunque, the trees cannot be cut down and other activities are limited.

RIVERS AND STREAMS

Puerto Rico has about fifty rivers and more than one thousand streams. Many of these waterways help provide water for the island's farms. The longest river, at about 46 miles (74 km), is the La Plata. It flows out of the Cayey Mountains, which are on the eastern edge of the Cordillera Central. The river then heads northward to the Atlantic Ocean. Other major rivers include the Grande de Añasco and the Loíza.

Some of Puerto Rico's rivers flow underground. The rushing water has carved out caves in the earth. One of these underground rivers is the Camuy, in the northwest part of the island.

Puerto Rico has no natural lakes, but a few artificial lakes were created during the twentieth century. Dams built across rivers created these lakes. These artificial lakes provide water for farming. Some are also used for boating and other types of water recreation.

Lake Guayabal in southern Puerto Rico is popular with fishermen.

Some of the waters off the coast of Puerto Rico have a special attraction. The island has several bioluminescent bays. The bays' waters seem to glow with a greenish light. This light comes from tiny creatures called dinoflagellates that live in the bays. When the creatures are disturbed, they begin to glow.

CLIMATE

Puerto Rico has a tropical climate. The weather stays mild all year round. The average summer temperature is 80° Fahrenheit (27° Celsius), while the average winter temperature is 73° F (23° C). In 1979, Puerto Rico had its highest recorded temperature, 106° F (41° C) in Lajas. The record low of 40° F (4° C) occurred at Adjuntas on March 3, 1993. In general, the southern coast tends to be slightly warmer than the northern coast.

Southern Puerto Rico is also the drier part of the island. This region gets less than 37 inches (94 cm) of rain per year. The north gets about 70 inches (178 cm) per year. In the rain forest the air is thick, and up to 240 inches (610 cm) of rain falls every year. In general, the mountain regions are slightly cooler than the coasts.

The Caribbean region is often hit with hurricanes. These powerful storms have strong winds and create large, damaging waves. Hurricanes form over warm areas of the Atlantic Ocean and move toward the

Caribbean and North America. These storms usually occur between June and November.

Puerto Rico sits in the path that many hurricanes take. Over the centuries, the island has been hit several times. A hurricane in 1899 killed three thousand Puerto Ricans. In 1998, Hurricane Georges destroyed buildings and land across the island.

FIND OUT MORE

The word *hurricane* comes from the word *Jurakán,* the Taíno word for a storm god. What is another name weather forecasters use for hurricanes?

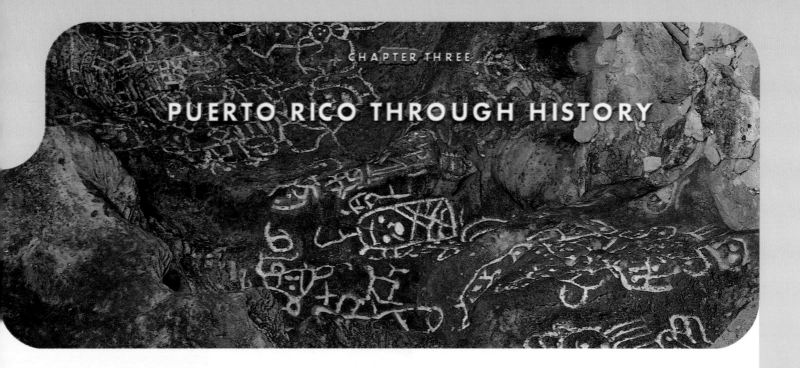

CHAPTER THREE

PUERTO RICO THROUGH HISTORY

Puerto Rico's earliest people created these petroglyphs, or rock drawings, near Arecibo.

Thousands of years before people discovered Puerto Rico, various animals roamed the island. Many of these creatures were much larger relatives of animals found today. The three-toed sloth, for example, is related to the giant ground sloth, which once roamed several islands of the Greater Antilles. This ancient sloth could grow as large as an elephant.

More than five thousand years ago, native people of South and Central America sailed to Puerto Rico and neighboring islands. The first settlers lived close to the coast. They mostly fished for their food, though some Native Americans hunted birds and turtles using stone weapons. Different groups of these Native Americans came to the islands at different times.

The last major group to reach Puerto Rico was the Taíno. They reached the island about twelve hundred years ago. Before then, the

Taíno most likely lived on other islands in the Caribbean. They called their new home *Borikén,* which means "land of the brave lord." Today, descendants of the Taíno on Puerto Rico still use this name.

The Taíno lived in villages spread out across the island. Up to several thousand people could live in one village. They built huts made of wood and straw called *bohíos.* These simple huts were strong enough to survive fierce hurricanes. For food, the Taíno mostly farmed. Their main crops included corn and yucca, a tropical plant. Yucca roots were used to make food. The Taíno made pots and other items out of clay. Some skilled workers made jewelry out of gemstones, gold, and shells. The Taíno also had a formal religion and were ruled by chiefs called *caciques.* Women were considered the equal of men and could serve as cacicas.

The Taíno lived a peaceful life, but they did have one enemy. Natives called the Carib had come from South America to the West Indies. They attacked Puerto Rico and other islands where the Taíno lived. The Taíno defended themselves with spears, but the Carib won many battles. Sometimes the Carib took Taíno women and children as slaves. Then, at

Evidence of the Taíno can be found in Utuado, where the remains of ten Indian courts are located. Dating from about A.D. 1100, they may have had religious significance.

the end of the 1400s, the Taíno had another threat to their peaceful life—the arrival of Europeans.

THE SPANIARDS ARRIVE

In 1492, a navigator named Christopher Columbus sailed west from Spain across the Atlantic Ocean. When he reached the West Indies, he claimed the islands he found for Spain. Europeans called these lands "the New World." The next year, Columbus returned to the West Indies. On November 19, 1493, the explorer reached Puerto Rico. He named the island *San Juan Bautista*—Spanish for "St. John the Baptist."

Christopher Columbus sailed to the Caribbean and South America four times between 1492 and 1504.

Puerto Rico was now a colony of Spain. A colony is a territory ruled by a powerful nation. Food, minerals, and other natural resources from the colony are often used for the benefit of the ruling nation.

About 30,000 Taíno lived on Puerto Rico when Columbus arrived. The explorer and his men did not have much contact with the Taíno. Columbus stayed long enough to get food and water, then sailed on to a neighboring island he had reached on his first trip to the West Indies. For several years, Spanish ships seldom came to Puerto Rico. Instead, they went to other colonies where settlers had built homes and begun to look for gold and silver.

The first Spanish settlers arrived in Puerto Rico in the summer of 1508. The Spanish explorer Juan Ponce de León arrived with about forty people. Ponce de León later wrote, "From the sea, the port and island looked exceedingly good." The settlers hoped to find gold on the island. They started a town called Caparra near San Juan Bay. For shelter, they built one large house.

Ponce de León became the first governor of Puerto Rico. He and Spain's rulers believed they could do whatever they wanted on Puerto Rico. They took all the gold they

(opposite)
La Fortaleza and the city walls, as well as other fortifications, protected the city and the Bay of San Juan from enemy attack.

found. The Spaniards also forced the Taíno to work as slaves. The Taíno could no longer do what they liked. They had to work on Spanish farms and mine for gold. They were punished if they did not obey the Spaniards or tried to escape. Many Taíno died working as slaves; others died from diseases the Spaniards brought with them to the West Indies. The Taíno tried to rebel in 1511, but the Spanish soldiers had better weapons and quickly ended the rebellion.

The Spaniards also brought in slaves from Africa. The slaves grew sugarcane for their masters. Spanish men often had children with their Taíno and African slaves. These children were called *mestizos*. The mestizos had one Spanish parent and one African or Native American parent. White Spaniards, however, controlled the island.

The Spaniards quickly mined all the gold on the island. Spain's leaders then saw another role for Puerto Rico: It became an important base for the Spanish navy. The island was close to other Spanish colonies, and ships could easily sail into its ports. By 1521, the Spaniards had a safe harbor in San Juan. The city had first been called Puerto Rico, or "rich port." Around this time, the harbor town was called San Juan and the entire island was called Puerto Rico. From San Juan, Spain could defend its other colonies in the West Indies. In 1533, the Spaniards began building a fortress in San Juan called La Fortaleza. This and other forts helped the Spaniards defend Puerto Rico from enemy attack.

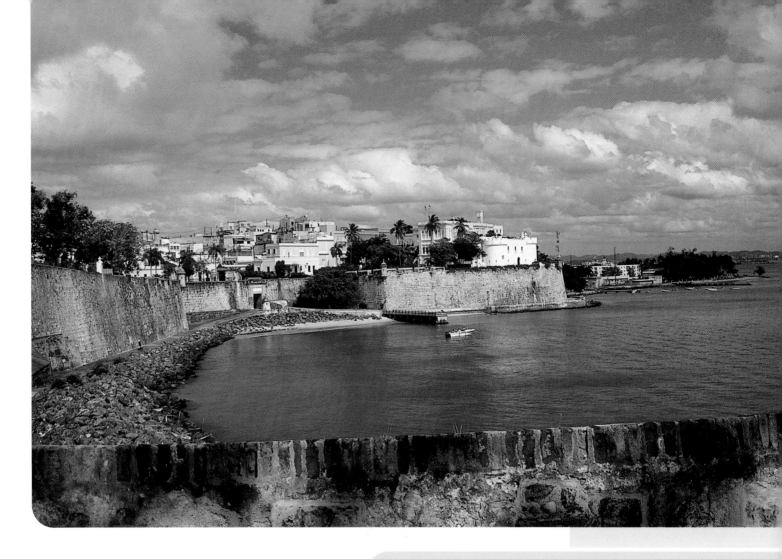

Despite the forts, other European countries tried to invade Puerto Rico. The French, English, and Dutch sent warships at different times. They also had colonies in the West Indies, and they wanted to use San Juan as a port for their ships. The French never landed on Puerto Rico, but troops from England and the Netherlands (the

WHAT'S IN A NAME?

The Taíno and Spanish languages shaped the names of many places in Puerto Rico.

Name	Comes From or Means
Borikén	Taíno for "land of the brave lord"
Caguas	From Caguax, the name of a Taíno chief
Mayagüez	Taíno for "place of many waters"
San Juan	Spanish name for St. John the Baptist
Puerto Rico	Spanish for "rich port"

This illustration shows a map of Puerto Rico around 1599.

Dutch) did. In 1598, the English held San Juan for almost three months. In 1625, Dutch troops controlled part of the island for almost a month. However, the Spaniards always won back their important colony.

CHANGING TIMES

During most of the 1600s and 1700s, Spain often ignored Puerto Rico and its people. Spanish rulers paid more attention to events in Europe and to its other colonies. Other times, Spain passed laws that hurt its colonies, but helped merchants in Spain. For example, Puerto Rico could sell its goods only to Spain. This law limited the growth of farming and other industries on Puerto Rico. The people had no reason to try to raise more crops or make more goods because they could not sell them wherever they wanted. Spain also required that all goods sail on ships leaving from San Juan. Some farmers had a hard time getting their crops to the city, and this also limited how much money they could make.

To earn more money, many farmers and merchants became smugglers. They illegally traded their goods with people on nearby islands. Towns along the coast were used as ports for smuggling ships. These towns included Aguada in the west and Fajardo in the east. The goods smuggled included sugar, tobacco, and livestock. They were traded for goods produced on other islands.

Spain finally saw that the economy of Puerto Rico was suffering. In 1765 it sent Alejandro O'Reilly to study the situation there. O'Reilly called the Puerto Rican people "the poorest that there are in America." The island had good crops and other resources, but the governor badly ruled Puerto Rico. O'Reilly also found just two elementary schools on the island outside San Juan. Few children outside of that city received any education.

As a result of O'Reilly's visit, Spain began to make some changes to improve life in Puerto Rico. It cut some taxes and let merchants trade with other Spanish islands in the Caribbean. The Spanish government also spent money to improve education and build new roads and bridges. By the early nineteenth century, Puerto Rico's economy was stronger. Fewer people had to smuggle to survive. Most Puerto Ricans, however, were still poor and could not read. Slavery also increased.

O'Reilly counted about 5,000 slaves in 1765. Most worked on farms, raising such crops as sugarcane, coffee, and cotton. In 1812, there were 17,536 slaves out of a total of 183,004 people. Increased demand for sugarcane led to the growth in slavery.

SEEKING INDEPENDENCE

By the early 1800s, Spain was no longer a powerful country. In 1808, France invaded Spain. French ruler Napoleon Bonaparte wanted to make his brother Joseph the king of Spain. For several years, the French and Spanish fought for control of the kingdom. For a time, part of Spain was ruled by Bonaparte's brother, and part was ruled by the Cortes. The Cortes was similar to the United States Congress—it made laws for Spain.

Spanish leaders in the Cortes tried to maintain control of Puerto Rico in the early 1800s.

During this time, people living in Spanish colonies saw how weak Spain had become. Many hoped to start revolutions and win their independence from Spain so they could rule themselves. To avoid a revolution in Puerto Rico, Spanish leaders decided to give the islanders some role in the government.

In 1809, for the first time ever, Puerto Ricans were allowed to vote in an election. They picked Ramon Power y Giralt to represent them in the Cortes. Three years later, the Cádiz Constitution was approved in Spain. Its extension to Puerto Rico gave Puerto Ricans essentially the same legal rights as people who lived in Spain. They could speak freely about public matters without worrying about being arrested, and people had the freedom to buy and sell property when they wanted. Puerto Ricans also soon won the right to trade freely with other countries.

The Puerto Ricans, however, soon lost many of their new rights. In 1814, Spain restored absolute power to the king. King Ferdinand VII then took away the rights Puerto Ricans and other Spanish citizens had gained in 1812. The Spanish governors in Puerto Rico once again assumed dictatorial powers. They had almost complete power over the Puerto Ricans. Anyone who seemed to be a threat to the new government was arrested or forced to leave the island. During this time, most Puerto Ricans lived as poor farmers, known as *jibaros.*

Many peasants lived in modest homes and owned only small pieces of land.

Meanwhile, wealthy Spaniards controlled the economy and owned slaves.

Some educated Puerto Ricans saw how hard life was for most people on the island. A few of these people wanted some control over how Puerto Rico was run. Some also wanted to remain part of Spain. Others, however, wanted complete independence for the island.

One of the leading supporters of independence was Ramón Emeterio Betances. A doctor, Betances had helped treat sick people during an outbreak of cholera in 1855. This disease affects the stomach and can be deadly if it is not treated quickly. Betances was later forced out of Puerto Rico because he opposed the leaders of the island. They did not accept his demands for independence. In 1864, Betances called for a revolution. He wrote, "Let us join together, and rise . . . against the oppressors of our land, of our women, and our children."

On September 23, 1868, supporters of Betances launched a revolution. About six hundred people took over the town of Lares and declared Puerto Rico's independence. The rebels arrested the town's mayor before marching on to Pepino. At Pepino, government troops attacked and forced the rebels to flee. By the end of December, government forces had captured almost all of the rebels. About ten were killed and twenty escaped. This failed revolution was known as *El Grito de Lares*—"the Cry of Lares."

Slowly, some changes came to Puerto Rico. Slavery was outlawed in 1873. Most of the freed people worked on farms, as they had done as slaves. A few skilled slaves left to take jobs in cities and larger towns. Most free blacks and mestizos, however, still lived in poverty—they lacked enough money to pay for decent food, clothing, and housing.

In the nineteenth century and the first decades of the twentieth century, many Puerto Ricans lived in small rural villages like this one.

Tobacco was one of Puerto Rico's most important crops, after sugarcane and coffee.

To help the farm owners who lost slaves, the government gave them money. However, it was not enough to pay for new workers. By this time, coffee was replacing sugarcane as the island's main crop. Farmers from Europe brought modern ways of growing coffee and preparing it for sale. The coffee farmers on the island did well, compared to people who raised sugarcane or other crops. Growing tobacco and making cigars also provided some jobs during this time.

During the 1870s and 1880s, people who shared ideas about how Puerto Rico should be ruled formed groups called political parties. The different parties chose people to run in local elections. The parties did not always agree about what kind of relationship Puerto Rico should have with Spain.

In 1887, the Autonomist Party was formed. This party wanted autonomy for Puerto Rico. This meant the island would still belong to Spain, but it would have its own government that could make laws. Most party members did not favor a revolution to win complete independence from Spain. Luis Muñoz Rivera, a party leader, wrote, "Let us live in friendly separation." He thought Puerto Rico could keep good relations with Spain while gaining more freedom to do what it wanted. Puerto Rico's leaders opposed the Autonomist Party, and many members were arrested and tortured.

During the 1890s, Muñoz Rivera united the Autonomist Party with the Liberals, a party in Spain. When the Liberals came to power in 1897, they granted Puerto Rico its autonomy. A new government elected by island residents took power on July 17, 1898. Just days later, Spain's role in Puerto Rico ended. A new country was about to take over.

EXTRA! EXTRA!

Workers in cigar factories were considered more skilled than other factory workers, so they received better pay. They also had a benefit other factory workers did not have—as the workers made cigars, someone read to them from local newspapers or books. Since many Puerto Ricans could not read, this helped them learn while they worked.

UNITED STATES CONTROL

Spain and the United States had gone to war in April 1898. At the time, another island about 500 miles (805 km) west of Puerto Rico, Cuba, was a Spanish colony. The Cubans were fighting for their independence, and the United States wanted an end to the fighting. Yet the government also

WHO'S WHO IN PUERTO RICO?

Luis Muñoz Rivera (1859–1916) was a journalist and a politician. He served as the secretary of state and chief of the cabinet of the newly independent Puerto Rican government. When Puerto Rico came under United States rule, Muñoz Rivera traveled to Washington, D.C., to fight for the rights of Puerto Ricans. He wanted the people to have autonomy and choose their own leaders. Muñoz Rivera was called "the George Washington of Puerto Rico." Like Washington, he fought for freedom against a foreign country, though Muñoz Rivera used words—not guns—in his battle.

wanted Cuba to win autonomy from Spain. Americans owned many farms in Cuba, and the United States government wanted to protect their interests. The island was an important source of sugarcane. American leaders hoped to play a larger role in the island's affairs.

The Spanish-American War began after a United States naval ship, the *Maine,* blew up in Cuban waters. Some Americans accused Spain of destroying this ship. (Historians now believe an accident on the ship probably caused the explosion.) The loss of the *Maine* led the United States government to declare war against Spain.

The United States officially declared war against Spain in April 1898. Major naval battles took place in the Philippines and off the coast of Cuba.

U.S. soldiers arrived in Puerto Rico to fight the Spanish troops stationed there during the Spanish-American War.

The United States military soon attacked several Spanish colonies around the world. On July 25, 1898, U.S. troops landed on Puerto Rico. They easily defeated the few Spanish troops on the island. A few days later, a United States general told the Puerto Ricans that Americans had come "to bring you protection . . . and to bestow upon you the . . . blessings of the liberal institutions of our government."

The United States quickly won the Spanish-American War. In December 1898, the country officially took control of Puerto Rico. Some American leaders believed it was good for the United States to have colonies around the world. American companies could control the natural resources in the colonies. Puerto Rico also gave the U.S. Navy an important port. Ships could come to the island for supplies and fuel. From Puerto Rico, they could easily sail to countries in South America.

American leaders did not think Puerto Ricans were able to rule themselves, and so the first United States government on Puerto Rico was run by the military. In 1900, a law called the Foraker Act ended military rule, but the United States still controlled the island's government and economy.

This illustration shows the city and harbor of Ponce in the 1890s.

American leaders made improvements on the island. They built schools, roads, and hospitals. Still, many Puerto Ricans were upset that they had lost control of their land. U.S. businesses began to take over the island's farms. Americans spoke a different language and had a different culture. Puerto Ricans also disliked the attitude of Americans, many of whom looked down on the Puerto Ricans. Luis Muñoz Rivera wrote, "Within a half a century, it will be a disgrace to bear a Spanish [name]." The United States even changed the spelling of the island's name to Porto Rico.

In 1917, Congress made Puerto Ricans United States citizens, but they still lacked an important right—the people could not choose their own governor. Some Puerto Ricans did not even want to be U.S. citizens—they wanted complete independence.

Life for many Puerto Ricans remained hard. The island lacked many high-paying jobs, and the typical family earned just a few hundred dollars per year. Large American companies owned many of the island's businesses. Most of the money these companies made went to the United States. The money did not stay in Puerto Rico, where it might have been used to help the people.

OPERATION BOOTSTRAP AND BEYOND

The poverty of Puerto Rico worsened during the 1930s. This was the time of the Great Depression. In 1929, the value of stocks that people

33

owned in U.S. companies began to fall. As people lost money, they rushed to banks to take out their savings. Many banks did not have enough money to give everyone what they wanted. As a result, many people did not have enough money to buy basic goods or other products. Companies lost sales and began to fire workers. Many people lost their homes and struggled to find food.

In Puerto Rico, the difficult economic times led members of the Nationalist Party to call for a change in government. The Nationalists were a political party that wanted independence. They were led by Pedro Albizu Campos. He said, "What is needed is a rebel organization . . . to make a clean break with [the United States]." Violence sometimes broke out between the government and the Nationalists. In 1937, twenty people were killed by the police in Ponce in what came to be called the Ponce Massacre.

Despite the problems caused by the Great Depression, Puerto Rico saw some improvements. In 1938, Luis Muñoz Marín helped start

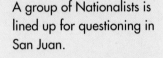

A group of Nationalists is lined up for questioning in San Juan.

34

the Popular Democratic Party (PDP). A favorite PDP saying was "Bread, Land, and Liberty." The party hoped to give Puerto Ricans more food (bread), their own farms (land), and freedom to run their own government (liberty).

Over the next few years, Muñoz Marín worked closely with Rexford Tugwell, the American governor of the island. The government brought electricity and running water to isolated parts of the island. Some poor farmers also had their first chance to own land. Before this, many worked on farms owned by the wealthy. Muñoz Marín also finally convinced United States leaders to let Puerto Ricans have more control over their own lives. In 1946, President Harry Truman named Jesús Piñero the governor of Puerto Rico. He was the first native of the island to hold that position. Two years later, Puerto Ricans elected their own governor for the first time. Muñoz Marín was an easy winner.

Muñoz Marín worked hard to end the island's poverty. He started a number of programs that together were called Operation Bootstrap. This name was based on an old American saying that people should pull themselves up by their bootstraps, which meant they should help themselves to improve their lives. Operation Bootstrap attracted new American companies to build factories in Puerto Rico. These factories made many items, including shoes, clothes, and clay products. Under the program, the companies paid few or no taxes, an arrangement much more attractive than if they built new factories in the United States. The island also offered plenty of workers and a good climate. The new

Many new factory jobs, such as this one in an automobile parts factory, were created in Puerto Rico during the mid-1900s.

FAMOUS FIRSTS

- Puerto Rican native Antonia Novello was the first woman and the first Puerto Rican to serve as U.S. surgeon general, taking office in 1990.
- The world's largest radio telescope, in Arecibo, sent its first message into space on November 16, 1974. The telescope is mostly used to detect radio signals in space.
- Herman Badillo was the first person born in Puerto Rico to represent part of the United States in Congress. He was elected to the U.S. House of Representatives in 1971 and represented part of New York City.

companies created jobs for Puerto Ricans. The island government also spent money to improve education, health care, and housing. Operation Bootstrap helped Puerto Rico reduce its poverty. Still, many Puerto Ricans faced a hard time finding good jobs, and thousands left the island for the United States.

Puerto Rico's relationship with the United States remained the most important issue for many islanders. In 1950, the

United States passed a law that let Puerto Ricans write their own constitution. Puerto Ricans drafted the document in 1951 and the U.S. Congress approved it the following year. On July 25, 1952, Puerto Rico became a commonwealth. Puerto Ricans remained United States citizens. They received all the legal rights outlined in the U.S. Constitution, such as the right to free speech and the right to receive a fair trial if they were accused of a crime. But they did not have to pay the United States income tax. This is money the government collects based on how much money a person earns each year.

However, this new relationship with the United States also placed some limits on their rights. Puerto Ricans could not vote in presidential elections. They also did not have representatives in Congress who could vote on United States laws.

Many Puerto Ricans welcomed this new relationship. They believed Puerto Rico had more autonomy as a commonwealth than it would have as a colony or a state. Others, however, wanted either statehood or independence. As a state, Puerto Rico would have voting members of Congress. It would also receive more money from the U.S. government than it would as a commonwealth. Nationalists and pro-independence groups

The flag of the Commonwealth of Puerto Rico stood beside the United States flag for the first time in 1952.

believed the island should become an independent country. Then it could follow its own ideas on every issue.

When Puerto Ricans have been consulted in different types of elections, more than half the voters favored remaining a commonwealth. Most of the rest favored statehood. A smaller number of voters supported independence.

RECENT HISTORY

Puerto Rico's economy continued to grow after Operation Bootstrap. More people worked in factories and stores and fewer worked on farms. A new U.S. law continued to reduce taxes for American companies that made goods on the island. Puerto Rico became wealthier than most nations in the West Indies. Still, Puerto Rico's wealth lagged behind the wealth of the United States.

In politics, Puerto Ricans remained split between people who wanted statehood and those who liked the commonwealth. During the 1990s, Puerto Ricans voted several times on what kind of government they wanted. In 1993, a majority of voters chose to keep the commonwealth. Another vote five years later did not lead to any change. Some Puerto Ricans still feel their island is a colony, but the people cannot agree on how it should be ruled.

A group of Puerto Ricans rallied for independence before the 1993 vote.

A new problem between the United States and Puerto Rico soon arose. Many Puerto Ricans protested the United States Navy's activities on parts of the island of Vieques. Since the 1940s, the navy has occupied about two-thirds of the island. Up to 2003, sailors and pilots used this land to practice firing weapons. In April 1999, a Puerto Rican was accidentally killed on Vieques. The protests caused the navy

The U.S. Navy conducts training exercises on Vieques.

WHO'S WHO IN PUERTO RICO?

Sila Maria Calderón (1942–) worked in business and served as mayor of San Juan before becoming the governor of Puerto Rico. As governor, she called for the U.S. Navy to leave Vieques, a position that was popular with many Puerto Ricans. She also called for new government spending to fight poverty on the island. Her plan would build new homes and create new jobs.

to reduce its military exercises there. After much public pressure, the navy was scheduled to end military practices by May 2003.

In 2000, Puerto Rican voters made history. They elected Sila Maria Calderón as the island's first female governor. Calderón wanted to keep Puerto Rico a commonwealth. She said, "Commonwealth allows us to conserve our Puerto Rican identity." The issue of how Puerto Rico should be ruled will probably not be settled soon.

CHAPTER FOUR

GOVERNING PUERTO RICO

For many years, Puerto Rico was governed by foreign nations. Spain named the governors who ruled the island when it was a Spanish colony. From 1898 until 1948, the United States also sent its own governors to rule. Since 1952, Puerto Rico has been a United States commonwealth. This kind of government has given Puerto Ricans more control over their island. The people now choose their own governor. The United States, however, still plays a major role in Puerto Rican affairs.

To understand how Puerto Rico is different from the states, take a closer look at how the United States government works. The government is made up in part by representatives from each state. Each state elects members to the United States Congress, the lawmaking body of the United States. Congress has two parts, called houses—the House of Representatives and the Senate. The number of members each state elects to

Murals inside the capitol dome illustrate the history of Puerto Rico.

the House is based the state's population. In other words, larger states have more representatives. Each state—no matter what the population—elects two members to the Senate. Members of Congress write documents called bills. These bills contain the wording for new laws for the country. A bill must be approved by both Congress and the president to become a law.

As a commonwealth, Puerto Rico differs from the states. Puerto Rico does not have representatives or senators in Congress. Its voters elect a resident commissioner to represent them in Congress. This person can vote within the committees that write bills. However, the resident commissioner cannot vote to approve or reject these bills.

Puerto Ricans also cannot vote for the United States president. Puerto Ricans who move to the United States can register to vote in presidential elections. They must also pay federal income taxes.

THREE BRANCHES OF GOVERNMENT

In 1952, the United States Congress approved a constitution for Puerto Rico. That document is still used today. For the most part, Puerto Ricans govern themselves, but the United States has control of key areas such as defense, foreign relations, and others. Under its constitution, Puerto Rico has a government similar to the United States system. The government is split into three parts, or branches. They are the legislative, executive, and judicial.

Legislative Branch

The legislative branch makes the laws of Puerto Rico. Puerto Rico's legislative body is called the Legislative Assembly. Voters elect representatives to the Legislative Assembly. Each member serves for four years, a period called a term. Like the

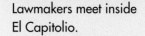

Lawmakers meet inside El Capitolio.

United States Congress, the Legislative Assembly has two houses. The House of Representatives usually has fifty-one members. The Senate usually has twenty-seven. At times, two extra seats may be added to either house.

Both senators and representatives serve for four years at a time. Most members represent a specific city or region, known as a district. Other legislators are elected as at-large candidates. This means they are chosen by voters on the whole island and represent everyone who lives there.

Anyone in the Legislative Assembly can propose a new law. A bill first goes to a committee in the House or the Senate, depending on where it was first proposed. The committee then lets the public offer an opinion about the bill, and may make changes to it. If the committee approves the bill, it must then be passed by both the House and Senate. The bill becomes law when the governor signs it. The governor may also veto, or reject, the bill. If so, the members of the Legislative Assembly can still make the bill a law if two-thirds of the members in each house approve it.

EXTRA! EXTRA!

Puerto Rico has one of the highest voter turnouts in the world. This means that most of the people who have registered, or signed up, to vote actually go to the polls. In the 2000 election, 82 percent of registered voters (82 in every 100 registered voters) cast a vote.

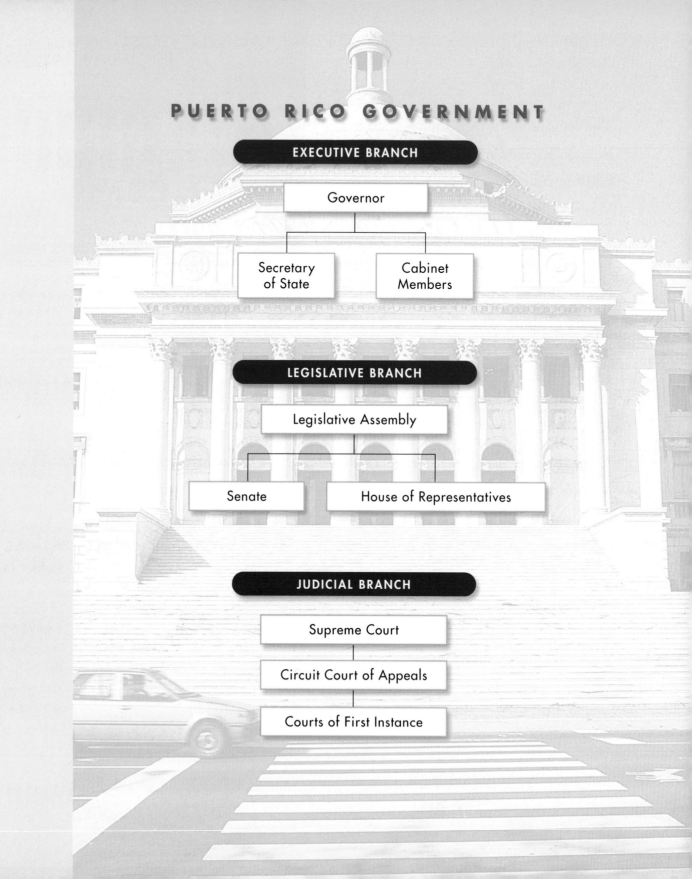

PUERTO RICO GOVERNMENT

EXECUTIVE BRANCH

Governor

Secretary of State

Cabinet Members

LEGISLATIVE BRANCH

Legislative Assembly

Senate

House of Representatives

JUDICIAL BRANCH

Supreme Court

Circuit Court of Appeals

Courts of First Instance

Executive Branch

The executive branch carries out the laws passed by the Legislative Assembly. The governor of Puerto Rico is the leader of the executive branch and is elected by the voters every four years. The governor selects

The governor's mansion stands by the waterside in San Juan.

most of the judges who serve on the island. He or she also picks people to lead departments that help the executive branch do its job. These department leaders are also part of the executive branch. The Legislative Assembly must approve these leaders and the judges. The governor also accepts or rejects laws passed by the legislative branch. During an emergency, the governor can declare martial law. This puts the military in control of the island.

After the governor, the most important person in the executive branch is the secretary of state. This person takes over as governor if the sitting governor dies or leaves office. The secretary also acts as governor if the governor travels away from Puerto Rico. Other executive positions include the Secretary of Justice (the lawyer for the government) and the heads of the departments of health, housing, education, and agriculture.

PUERTO RICO ELECTED GOVERNORS

Name	Term	Name	Term
Luis Muñoz Marín	1949–1965	Carlos Romero Barceló	1977–1985
Roberto Sanchez Vilella	1965–1969	Rafael Hernández Colón	1985–1993
Luis A. Ferré	1969–1973	Pedro Rosselló	1993–2001
Rafael Hernández Colón	1973–1977	Sila Maria Calderón	2001–

JUDICIAL BRANCH

The judicial branch interprets, or explains, the law. It determines the guilt or innocence of people accused of breaking the law. The courts also make sure Puerto Rico's laws do not violate the Constitution. The judicial branch includes all of the island's courts and the judges who serve in them.

Local cases are heard in what are called courts of first instance. These are the municipal, district, and superior courts. These courts of first instance hear cases that involve the breaking of laws, called criminal cases. They also hear cases that involve law-related disputes, or disagreements, between individuals. These are called civil cases.

After one of the lower courts makes a decision, the person involved may appeal, or challenge, the verdict. When a decision in a court is challenged, it goes to the circuit court of appeals. Thirty-three judges serve on this court. They serve sixteen-year terms.

If a decision by the court of appeals is challenged, it goes to Puerto Rico's highest court, the supreme court. The judge in charge of the supreme court is called the chief justice. Six other judges serve on this court.

Puerto Rico also has a United States District Court. This court hears cases involving United States laws. The judges for this court are appointed by the United States president. Cases heard in this court can be appealed to several higher U.S. courts, including the U.S. Supreme Court.

TAKE A TOUR OF SAN JUAN, THE CAPITAL CITY

Puerto Rico's capital is San Juan. Its population in 2000 was 434,374. San Juan is located on the island's northeast shore.

A bust of Christopher Columbus holding his ship, the *Santa Maria*, serves as a water fountain in Old San Juan.

San Juan is divided into districts. Most tourists flock to Old San Juan, where the Spaniards first settled in the city. This district has most of the city's historic buildings. The United Nations has named Old San Juan one of the world's most important historic areas.

Puerto Rico's governor lives in Old San Juan at La Fortaleza. This building was first used as a fortress to protect Spanish settlers from attacks by other Europeans exploring the Caribbean. La Fortaleza is the oldest governor's house still used as such in North and South America.

Other historic buildings line the streets and waterfront of Old San Juan. Starting in the sixteenth century, El Morro Castle was used by the Spanish to defend San Juan from enemy attack. Today the fort has a museum featuring armor and weapons hundreds of years old. Across Old San Juan is another famous fort, San Cristóbal. The Spanish began building it in the 1630s, and construction continued for more than one hundred years. When United States troops invaded

More than two million visitors come to El Morro each year, making it Puerto Rico's best-known fortress.

Puerto Rico in 1898, Spanish defenders fired their first shots from San Cristóbal.

Old San Juan also has a number of historic Roman Catholic churches. San José Church was built in 1532. It is said to be the second oldest church in North and South America.

The districts outside of Old San Juan also have notable buildings. One newer district is Puerta de Tierra. There, Puerto Rico's lawmakers work at a building called El Capitolio. Nearby is Condado, a popular

EXTRA! EXTRA!

Even the streets of Old San Juan are historic. They are paved with bluish stone bricks called *adoquines*. In the 1500s, Spanish ships carried these stones for extra weight.

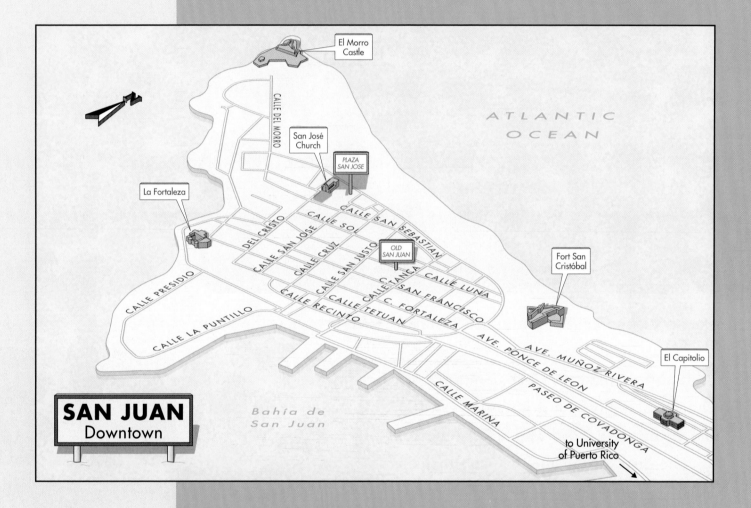

El Morro
Castle

ATLANTIC
OCEAN

San José
Church

PLAZA
SAN JOSE

La Fortaleza

CALLE DEL MORRO

CALLE SAN SEBASTIAN

DEL CRISTO

CALLE SOL

CALLE SAN JOSE

CALLE CRUZ

OLD
SAN JUAN

Fort San
Cristóbal

CALLE SAN JUSTO

CALLE LUNA

C. TANCA

CALLE SAN FRANCISCO

CALLE PRESIDIO

C. FORTALEZA

CALLE TETUAN

CALLE LA PUNTILLO

CALLE RECINTO

AVE. MUÑOZ RIVERA

AVE. PONCE DE LEON

El Capitolio

PASEO DE COVADONGA

CALLE MARINA

Bahía de
San Juan

to University
of Puerto Rico

SAN JUAN
Downtown

tourist stop. The area lies along the beach, and hotels and small shops line the streets. East of this area is Santurce. This district has an arts center with three theaters for live performances.

San Juan has one of the busiest ports in the Caribbean and is a business center for the region. Most of the largest banks and office buildings are in a district called Hato Rey. One street lined with modern businesses and stores is nicknamed "the Golden Mile."

South of the business center is Río Piedras. This is the home of the main branch of the University of Puerto Rico. The school was founded in 1903 and now has eleven branches across the island. As of 2001, more than 21,000 students attended the university in Río Piedras. The school there has a huge variety of plants and flowers on display at its botanical garden.

Farther west is Cataño, home of the world's largest plant (factory) for making rum. The plant belongs to the Bacardi family. They first began making

WHO'S WHO IN PUERTO RICO?

Ivan Rodríguez (1971–), nicknamed "Pudge," played for the Texas Rangers and quickly became one of the greatest catchers in baseball. He has won ten Golden Glove awards, which are given each year to the best fielder at each position. He was also named the 1999 Most Valuable Player in the American League. Rodríguez now has a home in Río Piedras, and he often donates money to worthy causes on the island. Rodríguez was born in Vega Baja, a town outside San Juan.

The University of Puerto Rico in San Juan opened in 1903 as the first public university in Puerto Rico.

this liquor from molasses during the 1800s in Cuba. During the 1930s, they opened their plant in Cataño. At full operation, the plant can make 100,000 gallons of rum every day.

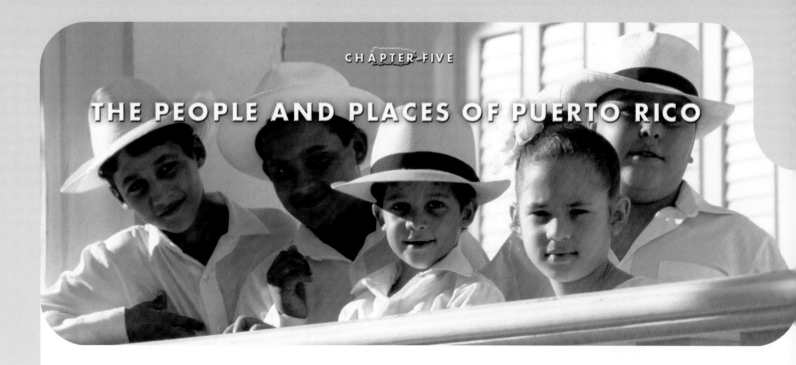

CHAPTER FIVE

THE PEOPLE AND PLACES OF PUERTO RICO

The people of Puerto Rico come from many different backgrounds. They have created a special culture for their island. Still, no matter how different Puerto Ricans may be, they share a pride in their beautiful island home.

A group of children wearing traditional Spanish clothing pose outside in Ponce.

MEET THE PEOPLE

In 2000, just over 3.8 million people lived in Puerto Rico. On the island, about 7 in 10 Puerto Ricans live in a city. Most major cities are spread out along or near the island's coast. These include San Juan, Bayamón, Ponce, Carolina, and Mayagüez. Puerto Rico ranks as one the world's most densely populated areas. This

FIND OUT MORE

In 2000, about 3.4 million Puerto Ricans lived in the United States. Some of these people go back and forth between the United States and Puerto Rico, but some live permanently in the United States. What U.S. cities have the largest Puerto Rican population?

Spanish is most commonly used in Puerto Rico.

TAINO WORDS

These are some common English words with roots in the Taíno language.

Taíno	English
barbacoa	barbecue (process for roasting meat)
canoa	canoe (small boat)
hamaca	hammock (hanging bed)
iguana	iguana (small green lizard)
maraca	maracas (gourd instrument)

means that a large number of people live in a small area of land.

Almost all Puerto Ricans are Hispanic. Hispanic people come from a country or region that was once controlled by Spain. Puerto Ricans also trace their roots to other Europeans. About 8 in every 100 islanders call themselves black or African-American. A small number of people are distant relatives of the Taíno, the Native Americans who lived on the island when the Spanish first arrived.

The Spanish impact on Puerto Rico lives on in many ways. The strongest influence is the language. Many people speak both English and Spanish, but Spanish is more commonly used. The Spanish also borrowed some words from the Taíno, and these words were adopted by the English. The Spanish also brought the Roman Catholic religion to Puerto Rico. Once, almost all Puerto Ricans were Catholic. Today, some Protestant religions are spreading around the island, though Catholicism remains the most popular faith. Some Puerto Ricans also hold beliefs based on Taíno and African religions.

Religion is at the heart of many of Puerto Rico's festivals and in daily life. It plays a major role in art as well. Many resi-

A santero shows off his work at a craft fair.

dents keep *santos* in their homes. These are painted wooden statues carved to look like saints or other religious figures. Some santos are also made out of stone or clay. The artists who carve them are called *santeros*.

LIFE IN PUERTO RICO

Across Puerto Rico, people have many things in common. Once a year, towns and cities hold festivals for different Catholic saints. Each town or region has a particular saint that its citizens honor. More than seventy of these festivals are held each year. Other festivals celebrate local events or the

SPANISH LANGUAGE

The Spanish language is an important part of Puerto Rico's culture. These are some simple Spanish words and phrases and what they mean in English.

Spanish	English
¿Cómo está usted?	How are you?
Hasta mañana	See you tomorrow
Muchas gracias	Thank you very much
Perdóneme	Excuse me
Vámonos	Let's go

harvest season, whenever the major crop is ready to be picked. Puerto Ricans also celebrate all United States holidays, as well as some of their own. These extra island holidays include Discovery Day, November 19—the day Columbus reached Puerto Rico.

All the major festivals in Puerto Rico feature parades, music, dancing, and people in fancy masks and costumes. Puerto Ricans enjoy all kinds of music. Two styles that developed on the island are bomba and plena. Bomba was created by Africans brought to Puerto Rico as slaves. This dance music features drums. Plena, like bomba, is filled with fast rhythms, but other instruments besides drums are used. These include guitars, tambourines, and other small hand instruments that are shaken to create a sound.

Puerto Ricans in Old San Juan dance to bomba and plena at a street parade.

Food is also a major part of the festivals. Puerto Ricans enjoy a good meal even when they are not celebrating. Puerto Rican food blends many different cooking styles. The Taíno used chili peppers and other vegetables that are still part of Puerto Rican cooking. The Spanish brought to Puerto Rico some foods still common today, including garlic, potatoes, tomatoes, and plantains. Plantains are green-skinned fruits that are similar to bananas.

WHO'S WHO IN PUERTO RICO?

Tito Puente (1923–2000) was born in New York. He helped make popular salsa, a form of music played in Puerto Rico. Salsa combines rhythms found in Puerto Rican music with jazz. Puente was called "the king of salsa."

WORKING IN PUERTO RICO

The service industry makes up the largest part of Puerto Rico's economy. Jobs in this industry provide a service for people, such as financial services (money management), communications, and tourism. People in these fields also include office workers, educators, government employees, store workers, and many others. The island has stores and warehouses that sell the same kinds of goods found in the United States. The island also has its own banks and insurance companies.

Tourism is a key part of the service industry. Tourists—people who visit the island—eat at restaurants and stay in hotels. They also visit Puerto Rico's many historical sites, beaches, and cities. The workers who

Many Puerto Rican dishes start with a sauce called sofrito, which mixes tomatoes, spices, peppers, and onions. It is a basic ingredient in many stews and dishes featuring beans and rice. Here is a simple recipe for sofrito. Don't forget to ask an adult for help!

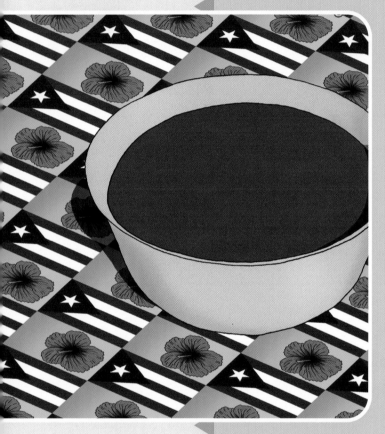

SOFRITO

2 bell peppers
2 tomatoes
1 medium-sized onion
3 cloves of garlic
recao leaves (use parsley if recao is not available)
cilantro
1 tbsp. cooking oil
1 tsp. annatto seeds

1. Chop the bell peppers, tomatoes, onion, and garlic.
2. Put the veggies in a blender or food processor, along with a few sprigs (leaves) of recao (or parsley) and cilantro. Blend until you have a paste.
3. Put cooking oil in a saucepan. Heat the oil, then add annatto seeds. Cook over low heat until the oil turns orange. Remove the seeds, then combine the oil with the mixed veggies.

take care of their needs make up the tourism industry. Visitors to Puerto Rico spend more than $2 billion each year.

The manufacturing industry—the making of goods—is almost as large as the service industry. Factories produce items such as clothes, electronic goods, plastics, and computer parts. Puerto Rican companies sell their goods to the United States and to other nations. The most important industry is the manufacturing of pharmaceuticals, or medical drugs. More than one hundred drug companies have plants (factories) on the island. The largest include Johnson & Johnson and Eli Lilly. Puerto Rico is also the world's leading producer of rum.

Puerto Rico is one of the world's top suppliers of pharmaceuticals, or medical drugs.

The United States has helped Puerto Rican industry by lowering taxes. By paying lower taxes, companies located there can afford to build bigger plants and hire more workers. These laws, however, will end by 2010. To prepare for the future, Puerto Rico hopes to attract more companies that rely on science and computers to create new products.

Once, most Puerto Ricans made their living as farmers. Today, farming makes up only a tiny part of the island's economy. The major crops include coffee, plantains, bananas, pineapples, mangoes, and citrus fruit.

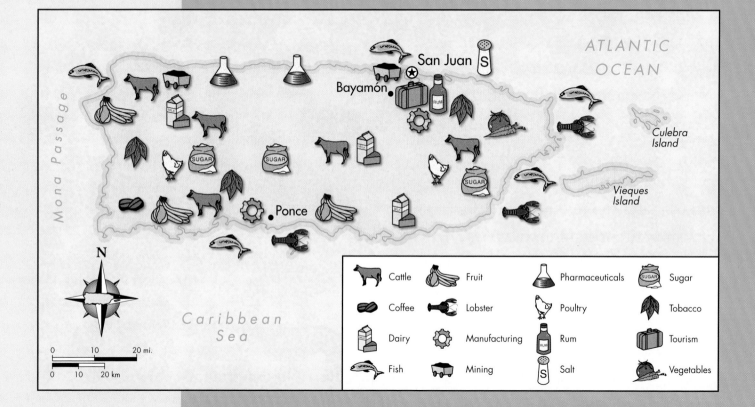

ATLANTIC OCEAN

Mona Passage

San Juan

Bayamón

Ponce

Culebra Island

Vieques Island

Caribbean Sea

N

0   10   20 mi.

0   10   20 km

Cattle		Fruit		Pharmaceuticals		Sugar
Coffee		Lobster		Poultry		Tobacco
Dairy		Manufacturing		Rum		Tourism
Fish		Mining		Salt		Vegetables

Farmers in Puerto Rico also raise a variety of animals. These include hogs and cows. Milk from the cows is used in dairy products. Chickens are raised for food and for their eggs.

The waters off Puerto Rico provide many kinds of fish that are sold in markets on the island and abroad. Tuna and lobster are particularly important. The value of all the fish caught each year is about $16 million.

A small number of Puerto Ricans work in mining. The materials mined include crushed stone, clay, and sand. Minerals used to make Portland cement are also mined. This cement is used to make a building material called concrete. Another mineral produced in Puerto Rico is salt. It comes from dried seawater.

TAKE A TOUR OF PUERTO RICO

Many visitors to Puerto Rico do not see much of the island. They are happy to stay in San Juan or at a hotel on the beach. These people miss some of the island's great history and fascinating charm. Here's a quick look at some of Puerto Rico's best sites and cities.

A rancher herds dairy cows near Toa Alto.

61

Western Puerto Rico

The major city of western Puerto Rico is Mayagüez. It has a population of about 98,434. Mayagüez is a major port. Ships sail from the city filled with fruit, sugar, and fish. The city has a branch of the University of Puerto Rico and is also home to the Tropical Agriculture Research Station. There, United States government workers raise a

Scientists at the Tropical Agriculture Research Station study problems related to tropical farming.

large variety of tropical plants. Visitors can tour the grounds and see more than two thousand tropical plants, including teak, rubber, and nutmeg trees. Mayagüez also has a beautiful city square lined with trees and statues.

Southwest of Mayagüez is San Germán. The town is located inland and is sometimes called City of the Hills. The Spanish first settled there in 1573. San Germán's Porta Coeli church was built in 1606, making it one of the oldest churches in the western hemisphere.

Central Puerto Rico

The western half of Puerto Rico's central region does not have any major cities. One important town is Utuado, with a population of about 36,000. Tourists often leave from there to visit nearby caves and forests. One popular spot is Rio Camuy Cave Park. The park has one of the largest systems of underwater caves in the world. Rivers running underground carved out the caves more than one million years ago.

Visitors peer into the depths of Rio Camuy Cave Park, carved out by the Camuy River more than one million years ago.

Isabela
Arecibo
ATLANTIC
OCEAN
Sabana
Seca   San Juan
Carolina
Loíza
Río Grande
2
2
22
22
2
Luquillo
Aguadilla
Bayamón
Guaynabo
Fajardo
Río Camuy
Cave Park
Caparra
Ruins
CARIBBEAN
NATIONAL
FOREST
CULEBRA
NATIONAL
WILDLIFE
REFUGE
Culebra
Island
Añasco
San
Sebastián
52
3
Isabel
Segunda
Mayagüez
Zoo
Utuado
Caguas
30
53
Mayagüez
52
Humacao
Vieques
Island
Coamo
52
Yabucoa
3
San
Germán
2
Ponce
1
52
53
3
3

Mona Passage

Caribbean Sea

N

0   10   20 mi.

0   10   20 km

National forest or
wildlife refuge

Highway

Capital city

City

Park (not all shown)

Tourist site

The city of Caguas lies in the eastern part of the central region. With a population of just over 140,000, it is the largest city in central Puerto Rico. Caguas is located in the Turabo Valley and is near El Yunque, or the Caribbean National Forest. Visitors come to the forest to explore its hiking trails and admire scenic waterfalls.

Southern Puerto Rico

The major city in the south is the port of Ponce. Its population in 2000 was 186,475. The city is a center for shipping and producing rum, coffee, and sugar. Ponce has many buildings that reflect the style of architecture found in Spain. The city also has one of the oldest volunteer firehouses on United States land. It is now used as a museum, featuring

Built in 1882, the unique red-and-black firehouse in Ponce is a city landmark.

WHO'S WHO IN PUERTO RICO?

Rita Moreno (1931–), born Rosita Dolores Alverio, is a popular singer, dancer, and actress. Moreno was the first person to win all four major entertainment awards: the Tony (for Broadway theater), Emmy (for television), Grammy (for music), and Oscar (for films). She won an Emmy for her appearance on "The Muppet Show." Moreno was born in Humacao.

old fire trucks and firefighting equipment. Another popular attraction is the Ponce Museum of Art. It displays works by both European and Latin American artists.

Eastern Puerto Rico

No major cities dot the east coast of Puerto Rico. The largest towns on or near the water are Humacao and Yabucoa. Near Humacao are fine beaches and resorts. The resorts offer tourists swimming, tennis, golf, and restaurants all at one location. Yabucoa is in a valley surrounded by green mountains. It is sometimes called the Sugar Town because of the nearby sugarcane fields. Each year the town has a sugar festival to honor that important local crop.

Off Puerto Rico's east coast are the islands of Vieques and Culebra. Tourists often spend relaxing days at the beaches on these islands. Vieques has only one town, Isabel Segunda. It features the last fort built by Spain in the Caribbean. Culebra was once used by the United States Navy for target practice by warplanes. Today, the island is a quiet spot for a tropical vacation.

Northern Puerto Rico

Not far from San Juan is the major city of Carolina. Its population in 2000 was 186,076. Carolina is home to many drug companies and to the island's one international airport. The city also has a sports center named for Roberto Clemente. This great athlete was the first Puerto Rican elected to baseball's Hall of Fame. Carolina also has several nice beaches.

Beachgoers walk along Flamenco Beach on Culebra.

Northeast of Carolina is the small town of Loíza. Many Africans lived there in the 1500s. Very few married the Spanish or other Europeans. Citizens of Loíza still have a strong African culture. Their annual festival is a popular event, featuring dances and parades. Loíza also features one of the oldest churches on the island.

Loíza's popular St. James Festival, held in July, includes colorful costumes and masks.

Also in the north is the city of Bayamón. This suburb of San Juan is Puerto Rico's second-largest city, with a population of more than 224,044. The city has a museum named for Francisco Oller, an artist from Bayamón. The city also has a science museum. Near Bayamón is the site of Caparra, the first Spanish town in Puerto Rico. A historical park in Caparra has ruins from the buildings constructed by Juan Ponce de Léon in the early 1500s.

On Puerto Rico's northwest shore is Arecibo. The city's population in 2000 was 100,131. Outside the city is the Arecibo Observatory. There, scientists search outer space for new stars and planets. The radio dish at Arecibo is the largest in the world. This radio dish has been used to listen for any signs of life on distant planets.

The 1,000-foot (305-m) radio dish in Arecibo is the largest in the world.

PUERTO RICO ALMANAC

Official name: Commonwealth of Puerto Rico, or Estado Libre Asociado de Puerto Rico

Date of commonwealth status: July 25, 1952

Seal: A lamb on a green circle, under a group of arrows. Also near the lamb are the letters *F* and *I,* which stand for "Ferdinand" and "Isabella," the rulers of Spain when Puerto Rico was discovered. Below the  lamb is the island's motto. Items around the green circle include castle towers, lions, crosses, and Spanish flags. These all relate to the early Spanish influence. The seal dates back to 1511 but was not officially adopted until August 8, 1952.

Flag: Three horizontal stripes of red alternating with two white stripes. A blue triangle on the left has a five-pointed white star on the inside. It was first used in 1895; officially adopted on March 3, 1952.

Geographic center: 18° 13.8' N and 66° 28.8' W

Total area 3,515 square miles (9,104 sq km)

Coastline: 311 miles (501 km)

Borders: Atlantic Ocean, Caribbean Sea; closest islands: U.S. and British Virgin Islands to the east; Hispaniola to the west

Latitude and longitude: Puerto Rico is located at approximately 18° 15' N, 66° 30' W.

Highest/lowest elevation: Cerro de Punta, 4,389 feet (1,338 m)/sea level along the coast

Hottest/coldest temperature: 106° F (41° C) at Lajas on October 25, 1979/40° F (4° C) at Adjuntas on March 3, 1993

Land area: 3,459 square miles (8,959 sq km)

Inland water area: 56 square miles (145 sq km)

Population (2000 census): 3,808,610

Population of major cities:

    San Juan: 434,374

    Bayamón: 224,044

    Ponce: 186,475

    Carolina: 186,076

    Caguas: 140,502

    Arecibo: 100,131

    Guaynabo: 100,053

    Mayagüez: 98,434

Origin of name: Spanish for "rich port," the original name of the city of San Juan

Capital: San Juan

Local government: 8 districts; 78 municipalities

U.S. representatives: One resident commissioner, a nonvoting member of Congress

Legislative Assembly: At least 51 representatives; at least 27 senators

Major rivers/lakes: Grande de Loiza, Bayamón, La Plata, Grande de Añasco/Guajataca

Farm products: Coffee, bananas, plantains, tomatoes, mangoes, eggs, dairy products, pineapples

Livestock: Poultry, beef cattle

Manufactured products: Pharmaceuticals, clothes, electronics, industrial machines

Mining products: Cement, crushed stone, salt

Fishing products: Shellfish, tuna

Official animal: Coquí, a tree frog

Official bird: Stripe-headed tanager

Official flower: Puerto Rican hibiscus

Motto: *Joannes Est Nomen Ejus* ("John is his name," referring to St. John the Baptist)

Nickname: Borikén (*Borinquen*, Spanish spelling)

Official tree: Silk-cotton tree, or ceiba

Wildlife: Coquí, iguana, Puerto Rican parrot, manatee

TIMELINE

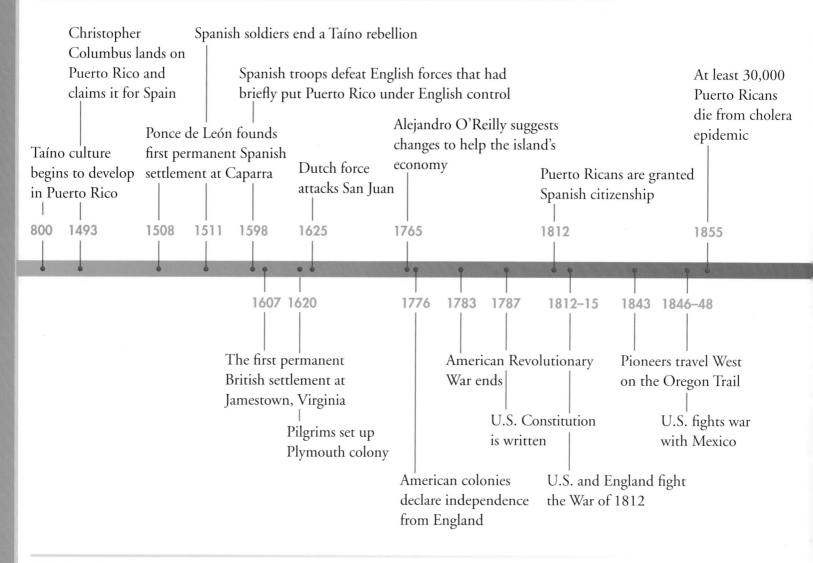

Christopher Columbus lands on Puerto Rico and claims it for Spain

Spanish soldiers end a Taíno rebellion

Spanish troops defeat English forces that had briefly put Puerto Rico under English control

At least 30,000 Puerto Ricans die from cholera epidemic

Ponce de León founds first permanent Spanish settlement at Caparra

Alejandro O'Reilly suggests changes to help the island's economy

Taíno culture begins to develop in Puerto Rico

Dutch force attacks San Juan

Puerto Ricans are granted Spanish citizenship

| 800 | 1493 | 1508 | 1511 | 1598 | 1625 | 1765 | 1812 | 1855 |

| 1607 | 1620 | 1776 | 1783 | 1787 | 1812–15 | 1843 | 1846–48 |

The first permanent British settlement at Jamestown, Virginia

American Revolutionary War ends

Pioneers travel West on the Oregon Trail

Pilgrims set up Plymouth colony

U.S. Constitution is written

U.S. fights war with Mexico

American colonies declare independence from England

U.S. and England fight the War of 1812

Spanish government ends
slavery on Puerto Rico

Rebels take over
Lares and declare
Puerto Rican
independence

The Jones Act grants U.S. citizenship
to Puerto Ricans

Puerto Rico becomes
a commonwealth
governed under its
own constitution

Puerto Ricans again
vote to remain a
commonwealth

U.S. troops land on
Puerto Rico; the island
soon becomes a U.S.
colony

Police in the
city of Ponce
kill protesters
who support
Puerto Rican
independence

Luis Muñoz Marín is
chosen as the first elected
governor of Puerto Rico

Sila Maria
Calderón
becomes
island's first
female
governor

1868   **1873** **1898**   **1917**   **1937**   **1948** **1952**   **1993** **2001**

1861–65   **1917–18** **1929**   **1941–45** **1950–53** **1964** **1965–73** **1969**   **1991** **1995**

U.S. takes part in
World War I

U.S. fights in
World War II

Civil rights laws
passed in the U.S.

U.S. and other
nations fight in
Persian Gulf War

U.S. fights in the
Vietnam War

Civil War
occurs in the
United States

The stock market
crashes and U.S.
enters the Great
Depression

U.S. fights in the
Korean War

Neil Armstrong
and Edwin
Aldrin land on
the moon

U.S. space
shuttle docks
with Russian
space station

GALLERY OF FAMOUS PUERTO RICANS

Julia de Burgos
(1914–1953)
This writer from Carolina published her first collection of poems in 1937. Her third book, *Canción de la Verdad Sencilla,* won a prize from the Institute of Puerto Rican Literature.

José Campeche
(1752 –1809)
Campeche taught himself how to paint by looking at copies of famous works of art. He became one of Puerto Rico's greatest artists. Born in San Juan.

Pablo Casals
(1876–1973)
Casals was a great cellist and conductor. He was born in Spain, but his mother was Puerto Rican. Casals moved to Puerto Rico in 1956 and helped shape classical music in Puerto Rico. A music festival named for him is one of the island's most important cultural events.

Ricky Martin
(1971–)
Martin, a native of San Juan, recorded several CDs in Spanish before releasing his first hit song in English. The song, "Livin' La Vida Loca," made Martin an international singing star.

Francisco Oller
(1833–1917)
Oller was Puerto Rico's most famous painter of the nineteenth century. He taught and won many awards for his artwork, which often featured the scenery and people of his homeland. Born in San Juan.

Luís Palés Matos
(1898–1959)
Palés Matos, from Guayama, was a descendent of African slaves brought to Puerto Rico. While still a teenager, he published his first book of poetry. He often wrote about the lives and problems of Africans living in the Caribbean. Some people consider him Puerto Rico's best poet of the twentieth century.

Antonia Pantoja
(1922–2002)
Pantoja spent many years in the United States helping to improve education for Puerto Ricans. In 1985, Pantoja returned to Puerto Rico and set up a program to help poor people who live in the countryside. Pantoja is one of only four Puerto Ricans to win the Presidential Medal of Freedom. Born in San Juan.

Esmeralda Santiago
(1948–)
One of the best-known Puerto Rican authors of recent years. Her most famous books, *When I Was Puerto Rican* and *Almost a Woman,* describe what it is like for Puerto Ricans who move between their native land and the United States. She spent her childhood in different parts of Puerto Rico, including Santurce.

GLOSSARY

adoquines: sixteenth-century bricks used to pave roads in San Juan

autonomy: freedom to make decisions with limited outside interference

bill: document created by lawmakers with a proposed law

bioluminescent: glowing with light made by living creatures

colony: territory ruled by a powerful nation for the benefit of the owning nation

commonwealth: the political status of Puerto Rico within the United States, granting the citizens some control over their own affairs

constitution: document that spells out the basic laws of a country, state, or commonwealth

Greater Antilles: group of islands in the Caribbean Sea that includes Puerto Rico

Hispanic: coming from a country or region once controlled by Spain

independence: when a nation and its people achieve full political control over its affairs

liberal: related to freedom and the legal rights of citizens

martial law: law enforcement carried out by the military

mestizo: person with one Spanish parent and one African or Native American parent

nationalist: person who supports independence for a colony

pharmaceuticals: drugs used for medicine

phosphorescent: producing light

plantain: green tropical fruit that is similar to a banana

poverty: the condition faced by people who lack money for appropriate food, clothing, and housing

rain forest: a forest that receives more than 100 inches (254 cm) of rain each year and features trees with high, thick leaves

resident commissioner: title of Puerto Rico's representative in the U.S. Congress

smuggle: trade goods illegally

trench: deep cut in the ocean floor

tropical: relating to a region of the world called the tropics, located north and south of the equator, that features a warm climate all year round

West Indies: group of islands located between the Atlantic Ocean and the Caribbean Sea

FOR MORE INFORMATION

Web sites

Welcome to Puerto Rico

http://welcome.topuertorico.org/

Information on Puerto Rico's history, culture, and arts.

Celebrating Hispanic Heritage

http://www.gale.com/free_resources/chh/index.htm

Explores Hispanic culture with biographies, activities, and a timeline.

El Boricua

http://www.elboricua.com/index.html

A Puerto Rican cultural site connected to a monthly magazine of the same name. Features a section for children.

Center for Puerto Rican Studies

http://centropr.org/

University-based institute that conducts research on Puerto Rican issues.

Puerto Rico Federal Affairs Administration

http://www.prfaa.com/eng/index.asp

Agency that serves as the U.S. presence of the government of Puerto Rico.

Books

Bernier-Grand, Carmen T. *Poet and Politician of Puerto Rico: Don Luis Muñoz Marín*. New York: Orchard Books, 1995.

Manning, Ruth. *Juan Ponce de León*. Chicago: Heinemann Library, 2001.

Márquez, Herón. *Destination San Juan*. Minneapolis: Lerner Publications, 1999.

Rudeen, Kenneth. *Roberto Clemente*. New York: HarperTrophy, 1996.

Silva Lee, Alfonso. *Coquí & His Friends: The Animals of Puerto Rico*. St. Paul: Pangaea, 2000.

Addresses

Caribbean National Forest
P. O. Box 490
Palmer, PR 00721

Puerto Rico Tourism Company
P. O. Box 902-3960
San Juan, PR 00902-3960

INDEX

ABOUT THE AUTHOR

Michael Burgan was an editor at *Weekly Reader* for six years. He created educational material for an online service and wrote about current events. Now a freelance author, Michael has written more than sixty books. He enjoys writing about history, geography, and famous people. To research this book, Michael used books, maps, newspapers, and the Internet. He found e-mail was useful for confirming information that was unclear in his sources. Michael also relied on the skills of friends who speak Spanish to help translate some information. Michael is a graduate of the University of Connecticut. He lives in Connecticut with his wife and their two cats.